PROJECTIVE GENOGRAMMING

Florence Kaslow, PhD

Director
Florida Couples and Family Institute
West Palm Beach, Florida

Professional Resource Press
Sarasota, Florida

Published by
Professional Resource Press
(An imprint of the Professional Resource Exchange, Inc.)
Post Office Box 15560
Sarasota, FL 34277-1560

Printed in the United States of America

Terry S. Proeger, PhD, served as Editorial Consultant for this book.

The copy editor was Patricia Hammond, the managing editor was Debra Fink, the production coordinator was Laurie Girsch, and the cover designer was Bill Tabler.

Library of Congress Cataloging-in-Publication Data

Kaslow, Florence Whiteman.
    Projective genogramming / Florence Kaslow.
       p. cm. -- (Practitioner's resource series)
    Includes bibliographical references.
    ISBN 1-56887-013-2 (pbk.)
    1. Family assessment. 2. Projective techniques. 3. Family-
-Psychological assessment. 4. Family-owned business enterprises-
-Succession--Plannng. I. Title. II. Series.
RC488.53.K38 1995
616.89'1--dc20   95-18287
                                         CIP

ACKNOWLEDGEMENTS

Appreciation and great respect are expressed to my (deceased) parents, Rose and Irving Whiteman, for creating a loving home in which they encouraged my sister, Cicely, and me to read and seek a fine education and to be part of our extended families of origin by telling us stories of earlier ancestors who had lived in Eastern Europe. Loyalty and adherence to tradition were clearly expressed values. Deep gratitude and admiration go to my husband of several decades plus, Solis Kaslow, who on my genogram appears as a true partner - in relating to both of our families of origin and in conceiving and rearing our two wonderful children, Nadine Joy and Howard Ian, whose very being has immeasurably enriched our lives and our reverence for the concept of "family" in its most positive of aspects. (Our venture into a family business is addressed later in this volume.) To our newest daughter (in law), Denise, and our next generation - our lovely granddaughter, Rachel Loren - our plaudits for the joy they bring. To all of these individuals, and the other "significant others" in my family of origin and creation, this guide is dedicated.

Special thanks are also expressed to my patient, kind, and understanding secretary, Gladys Adams, for typing and retyping this manuscript and for always being there for me.

PREFACE TO THE SERIES

As a publisher of books, cassettes, and continuing education programs, the Professional Resource Press and Professional Resource Exchange, Inc. strive to provide mental health professionals with highly applied resources that can be used to enhance clinical skills and expand practical knowledge.

All the titles in the *Practitioner's Resource Series* are designed to provide important new information on topics of vital concern to psychologists, clinical social workers, marriage and family therapists, psychiatrists, and other mental health professionals.

Although the focus and content of each book in this series will be quite different, there will be notable similarities:

1. Each title in the series will address a timely topic of critical clinical importance.

2. The target audience for each title will be practicing mental health professionals. Our authors were chosen for their ability to provide concrete "how-to-do-it" guidance to colleagues who are trying to increase their competence in dealing with complex clinical problems.

3. The information provided in these books will represent "state-of-the-art" information and techniques derived from both clinical experience and empirical research. Each of these guide books will include references and resources for

those who wish to pursue more advanced study of the
discussed topic.

4. The authors will provide numerous case studies, specific
recommendations for practice, and the types of "nitty-
gritty" details that clinicians need before they can incorporate new concepts and procedures into their practices.

We feel that one of the unique assets of the Professional
Resource Press is that all of its editorial decisions are made by
mental health professionals. The publisher, all editorial consultants, and all reviewers are practicing psychologists, marriage and
family therapists, clinical social workers, and psychiatrists.

If there are other topics you would like to see addressed in this
series, please let me know.

Lawrence G. Ritt, Publisher

FOREWORD

I have always been amazed by the variety of therapists who use genograms in their work. Although the family diagram was originally developed by Bowen to explore multigenerational family patterns, it has by no means remained a tool solely for one school of family therapy. I have found that therapists of all persuasions, whether structural, strategic, experiential, analytic, eclectic, integrative, and so on, have found the genogram useful. Even therapists who do not see families at all or ever think in terms of a system have told me they use genograms in their work. There is something compelling about having a map and cast of characters in *the* major drama of our lives: the unfolding of our family history.

When Monica McGoldrick and I wrote our book on genograms, it was our hope that a standard text, a conventionalization of the genogram symbols, and guidelines for interpretation would stimulate the use and development of the genogram. We tried to present the genogram in a general and nonsectarian manner that might be embraced or at least read by the largest possible cross-section of clinicians. Books like this one confirm this hope.

Freud saw the dream as the royal road to the understanding of the unconscious. It is fair to say that many family systems therapists see the genogram as the royal road to understanding the systemic and multigenerational context of the family. In this short but stimulating book, Florence Kaslow sees the genogram as the royal road to both the family system and the inner world of the individuals in that family. For her, the genogram becomes the supreme integrative tool. By having people do their own genograms with minimal instructions, and then free-associating about the result, the author stimulates and explores the deepest feelings and thoughts of family members. I found myself discovering new ways to use genograms. I believe the reader will as well.

Randy Gerson, PhD
March 1995

ABSTRACT

In the last four decades, the technique of genogramming has become popular in the field of family therapy. It affords an excellent opportunity for trainees and patients, as well as for senior clinicians and academicians, to explore their family connections - past, present, and future - as they perceive them to be and as they have been.

In this short guide, a derivative and expansion of traditional genogramming, designated "projective genogramming," is described. Its values are enumerated and case examples utilized to illustrate how it can be employed for maximum benefit. The intent of this monograph is to present an additional technique that clinicians can incorporate into their personal armamentarium of diagnostic and treatment tools. Its applicability in other contexts than the therapy setting is illustrated in a section on utilization in family business consultation when the focus is on succession planning.

TABLE OF CONTENTS

ACKNOWLEDGEMENTS   *iii*

PREFACE TO THE SERIES   *v*

FOREWORD   *vii*

ABSTRACT   *ix*

TRADITIONAL GENOGRAMMING   1

    Case #1   3
    Case #2   5

PROJECTIVE GENOGRAMMING: STEP ONE -
WITH WHOM DID YOU BEGIN AND WHY?   8

    Case #3 (Part A)   11
    Case #3 (Part B)   12

PROJECTIVE GENOGRAMMING: STEP TWO -
WHOM DID YOU OMIT OR EXCLUDE?   19

    Case #3 (Part C)   19

PROJECTIVE GENOGRAMMING: STEP THREE -
WHOM WOULD YOU LIKE TO ELIMINATE?   22

    Case #4   23
    Case #3 (Part D)   25

PROJECTIVE GENOGRAMMING: STEP FOUR -
WHOM WOULD YOU LIKE TO ADD?   26

    Case #3 (Part E)   27

USE OF THE PROJECTIVE GENOGRAM
IN FAMILY BUSINESS CONSULTATION   29

THE FINALE AND
POSSIBLE EPILOGUES   36

APPENDIX: GENOGRAM FORMAT   39

REFERENCES   41

PROJECTIVE
GENOGRAMMING

TRADITIONAL GENOGRAMMING

Genogramming has been a significant and frequently used technique in the field of family therapy. Its many advantages have contributed to its continued viability and use across time, for a span of several decades, and across space, as genogramming is popular in many countries around the world. Its universality gives it ongoing significance in this era of great concern for individual and familial differences within the context of multiracial, multiethnic, and multicultural pluralism. Everyone had or has a family of origin and perhaps also a family of creation. The symbols for depicting family members across generations can be the customary ones (McGoldrick & Gerson, 1985; see Appendix on pp. 39-40) learned by the majority of family clinicians, or idiosyncratic ones created between therapist and patient. Either way, the person drawing the genogram can determine the placement and configuration; this technique is not language-, race-, culture-, or gender-bound or -limited. This is one of the most compelling and elegant features of this technique.

In the pioneer generation of family therapists, Bowen (see Guerin, 1976 and F. W. Kaslow, 1982, 1987a, for historical accounts of the field), in particular, emphasized the centrality of family of origin (Bowen, 1978) and the importance of one's re-connecting in ways that facilitate dealing with the unfinished business from one's past. He developed the technique of geno-gramming as a way for patients to depict the individuals who comprise their historic past and present (Carter & McGoldrick, 1980). The typical instruction given to someone about to draw this form of a "family tree" was to "start as far back as you can remember." Most patients begin with their great-grandparents' or grandparents' generation, and the family tree descends from the top of the page from the senior progenitors to the youngest chil-dren in the clan. A chronological diagram emerges of how people are related to one another, and may contain such information as dates of birth, marriage, divorce, and death.

In order to do a reasonably complete genogram, one may embark on a journey to visit members of one's family of origin who are still alive to discover some of one's missing roots (Kerr & Bowen, 1988). The therapist coaches the person embarking on this type of investigation about what questions he or she might ask and how the person might want to interact with family members. In making this exploration, one may unearth long-buried family secrets; for example, discovering the existence of one or more relatives that no one has talked about for a long time. This proc-ess can be further facilitated by reviewing family photographs in the company of other relatives (F. W. Kaslow & Friedman, 1977; Weiser, 1993). When one starts sharing memories and querying, "Whatever happened to _____?", the key to a mystery may emerge.

The following concepts from Bowenian theory are particularly pertinent to projective genogramming. Often, the person doing the genogram will become aware of what Bowen called "the inter-generational transmission process"; that is, what has been passed on from "generation to generation" (Friedman, 1985) either overtly or covertly, physiologically and/or psychologically. For example, the individual doing the genogram can be asked to note on the genogram who in the family suffered from anxiety or depression, which relatives have had coronary conditions or cancer, who had a serious drinking problem, and so on, in order to collect data about physical and emotional family legacies. Such information also may illuminate the underlying reason for a particular source of apprehension or dread such as, "I won't live long, I'm bound to have a heart attack in the next few years." This fear is often predicated on the fact that the individual's father and paternal uncles all had coronaries in their forties. Interventions can then be aimed at eliminating the feeling of fatalism and powerlessness that has arisen in the individual's mind because "It's just what happens to the men in my family."

The genogramming process can also help someone become cognizant of a familial tendency to triangulate relationships. Such information might lead to discussions of how to detriangulate (Bowen, 1978) and could ultimately help the person doing the genogram to develop a more fruitful and satisfying interpersonal relationship system.

Let us consider a case that exemplifies some of the clinical benefits of genogramming for patient and therapist alike.

CASE #1*

Jerry had long heard about his marvelous paternal grandparents in southern Sweden and his Danish maternal grandmother, who had come with his parents to the United States before he was born. When he was old enough to inquire about his other grandfather, he received vague answers and gradually realized no one wanted to talk about this "grandpa." The veil of silence stimulated his curiosity.

Although this was not the main reason Jerry entered therapy, it was a theme that resurfaced periodically. When he had been naughty as a child or spunky and rebellious as an adolescent, he was chastised and sometimes told he was acting just like grandpa and worried them because, obviously, he was headed for trouble. Increasingly, Jerry felt he had to unravel the mystery; he felt his grandfather held a key to his own identity.

---

*Names and identifying characteristics of persons in all case examples have been disguised thoroughly to protect privacy.

When he was about to turn 25 years of age, his therapist encouraged him to go to Scandinavia and visit his ancestral home. He was coached on how to try to fill in the missing persons in his family tree. Fortunately, some of the extended family still resided in Sweden and Denmark and he was able to track them down. He spent some time visiting his maternal grandfather's aging brother and sister-in-law and their grown children. Photographs were pulled out and stories told of the family long ago in Copenhagen. Everyone commented on Jerry's uncanny resemblance to his grandfather; he saw how striking it was, too. He realized how much he must remind everyone of him, and so asked what he was like and why he had not emigrated to America with his wife and daughter. The initial response was an uncomfortable silence. Finally, Jerry's great uncle said his brother had been a "charming devil" who got involved in some unsavory business dealings, as well as with other women, and had so humiliated his wife in their community that she had decided to leave him and go as far away as possible, which is why she departed for the United States. Divorce was not an acceptable option and he would not leave town, so his wife had made a courageous decision and began life anew.

Jerry then understood why his grandmother never remarried. He also was struck by "huge bolts of lightning" as to why his parents and grandparents got so "uptight" when he did anything naughty, told little lies, or was described as "charming." They were terrified that he would end up like Grandfather Mangus.

He expressed his appreciation for their candor, as well as for the information provided. He asked if they would work with him to do a family genogram and suggested that they could fill in all they knew about the relatives in Denmark and he would sketch the American branch of the family. They were fascinated by the project and delighted with Jerry's promise that he would redo it when he got home, filling in additional data from his parents, and send them copies. Over the next 2 days they did the genogram and told stories about the people and their relationships as they were inserted into the family map. With the bounty retrieved from this voyage back into the family's historical past and the pleasures derived from sightseeing in his ancestral homelands of Sweden and Denmark, Jerry returned to America with a much clearer and stronger sense of his roots, heritage, and identity. He was able to interact with his parents with newfound respect for them and their parents in light of their heroic accomplishments in meeting the challenges of relocation to a very different culture.

The preceding anecdote illustrates how patients can use coaching from the therapist to undertake a voyage of discovery home in order to learn more about who they are and who their progenitors were (Bowen, 1978). If they ask questions to elicit the information they need about specific individuals and relationships, and place themselves in the intergenerational context, they may be able to access and connect to the multigenerational transactional system in such a way as to be able to work on comprehending and finishing some crucial "unfinished business from the past."

A very different case will be presented to show how using a traditional, Bowen-style genogram in therapy can be extremely valuable.

CASE #2

When Judy was in therapy with her relatively new second husband, Jim, and they were encountering myriad problems with their blended family, Judy was extremely sensitive about acknowledging that Jim was not the biological father of her two youngsters - Krista, age 1½ years, and Billy, a 3 year old. She wanted them to use Jim's last name so their surname would match hers and her husband's. Her ex-husband had abandoned the family abruptly in the middle of the night when Krista was 6 months old. The divorce had been bitter; the childrens' father sent no child support and had visited only once in a year.

Subsequently, when Judy pleaded with him to be more attentive to the children, he scoffed at her, saying, "You can't make me." Judy wanted to obliterate his memory and act as if he had never existed.

Jim was already extremely devoted to her children and willing to be a very involved stepfather. Nonetheless, he was unwilling to go along with a "let's pretend" charade. He had children from his first marriage and knew that he would never have wanted his paternity to have been denied. He realized that the children were entitled to know their biological father. Judy was infuriated by his attitude and interpreted it as uncaring. She believed he had married her and the children "as a package deal" and that he was reneging on a crucial part of the deal (F. W. Kaslow, 1993d).

In therapy, it was tactfully pointed out that her response seemed extreme and did not appear to fit with the current reality. Jim was a doting psychological daddy and had agreed that he would adopt the children after overtures to again find her ex-husband failed, and if he did not resurface in the next 3 years. She was livid with what she labeled a "foolish delay." However, she conceded, and they embarked on a year-long search to find Mr. X. He had vanished, as had support payments.

At the end of the carefully planned and prolonged search period, which was divulged to no one but their attorney and therapist, Jim agreed to adopt the children, have their names changed to his legally, and to collude to keep their biological father's role undisclosed. Judy was ecstatic, and the marriage and family fared well together. She terminated treatment because all was going well, and she was miffed at the therapist for suggesting possible future repercussions from this decision and the need for the children to have access to knowledge about the other half of their biological heredity.

When they returned to therapy years later, Jim reported he had experienced occasional discomfort when friends commented that neither of the children looked at all like him. He was always vaguely uneasy that somehow the children would find out, but had stopped voicing his concern to Judy as she became agitated and then dismissed his worries as "paranoid."

Some years after the adoption, Jim, Judy, and the two children had gone to a family reunion of Judy's extended clan. A cousin she hadn't seen in years asked Judy, in front of her son Billy, whether the children still saw their first father. Judy was flustered and sputtered out, "I don't know what you're talking about." Billy, now 11 years old, sensed his mother's embarrassment. He decided to wait until the ride home to ask what the cousin's question meant. He did, and when Judy attempted to mask the issue, Jim caught her attention and they silently decided that now was the time to tell the truth. Jim countered with, "We have a story to tell you." He explained as best he could, using language the children could understand easily. Once Judy recognized that the curtain of pretense had been pierced, she joined in. Both talked of how much they loved the children and were careful to indicate they did not know why Mr. X had disappeared and that they had diligently searched for him.

Since the children, particularly Billy, became upset at hearing the content of the revelation, the family resumed therapy for a few sessions to make certain the issue was dealt with sufficiently. Jim was relieved that the secret was out in the open. Genogramming was utilized to help the children see the various connections to each of their daddies and to help them comprehend the concept of a different biological and psychological father (Goldstein, Freud, & Solnit, 1973). The children liked working on this pictorial rendition of family connections, and asked to keep the genogram to help them understand. They also asked to see a picture of their "other daddy."

Billy insisted on knowing "why his mother and adoptive father had lied to him," stating logically, "You punish us if we do not tell the truth." Judy was assisted in explaining her desire to protect them and to really create a happy, stable home and family. When Billy, a perky and bright youngster, insisted that "mommy should be punished for lying," and his little sister chimed in about "parents having to obey the same rules as children," Judy and Jerry saw the wisdom of concurring. A ritual for appropriate "punishment" and forgiveness was devised, with all present participating in creating it (Imber-Black, Roberts, & Whiting, 1988). It was done at the next therapy session and the children were pleased that their concerns were heard, validated, and implemented. All seemed to draw closer and the parents conveyed that they had experienced an enormous wave of relief. Therapy was terminated by mutual agreement shortly thereafter.

The remainder of this monograph deals with a technique developed by this author called "projective genogramming." It describes the instructions and process that go into the graphic diagramming and some of the insights that may be derived from its utilization. In addition to case examples derived from clinical practice, one section addresses the applicability of the projective genogram in the field of family business consultation.

PROJECTIVE GENOGRAMMING: STEP ONE - WITH WHOM DID YOU BEGIN AND WHY?

About 16 years ago, when I was teaching a family therapy course at Hahnemann Medical University in Philadelphia, I explained the genogram symbols and told my students to draw their family. Inadvertently, I forgot to say "family of origin" and "start as far back as you remember" (i.e., the usual instructions for genogramming). All but two students proceeded to become engrossed in the project (more about them will follow later).

When we began discussing their family trees, what surprised me was that, given the freedom to proceed from an inner-directed logic and unconscious determinism rather than from an externally imposed structure, each person had started at the most significant and logical place for him or her. Each was amazed to find out that many of their classmates drew someone else first. What emerged was that each had begun with that person who was most pivotal in their current universe. Several drew themselves first, others a spouse, parent, grandparent, great-grandparent, sibling, or child. Pursuing why they started where they did by asking such questions as, "What is special about that person for you now?" led to wonderfully spontaneous, informative answers. Clearly, where they began was multidetermined and not pure chance.

Since that first "error," I now begin simply by saying "draw your family" and give no other directions or information. For me, over the past decade and a half, the genogram has become an excellent personal family projective assessment tool with myriad implications for the process and goals of treatment (F. W. Kaslow, 1986). It has proven valuable both in therapy and in the training of other therapists. This tool can be used in addition to such projective tests as the Thematic Apperception Test (TAT) and the Rorschach. Or it can be used alone, depending on the kind of information the therapist or trainee is seeking to elicit or impart.

When genograms are done using the more free-flowing projective format, feedback from workshop participants, ranging from novices to very experienced practitioners who are schooled and skilled in genogramming suggests that it is a most illuminating process and brings unknown or repressed patterns and connections into consciousness. It is not uncommon to have a therapist in a training setting or a patient say (Fay & Lazarus, 1984), "I've had so much therapy, including analysis, and we've never touched some of these core issues," or "Wow, this is amazing; I'm making so many important connections." The "aha" phenomenon may continue for weeks. Therapists as well as patients express similar reactions.

Occasionally some resistance may be encountered when one asks members of a family therapy/psychology class or participants in a workshop to "draw your family." Since the session when I first inadvertently assigned a projective genogram to my class over two decades ago, I have come to accept that those who refuse to do a projective genogram almost invariably have a solid personal reason for being resistant. As a consequence, they should not be pressured into complying. The main cause of their resistance appears to be that they know doing so will touch upon issues and feelings that either they are not ready to face or which will evoke more pain than they wish to deal with, especially in a group context. To elaborate further, I have had people who were adopted (as was true with one of the Hahnemann students) be embarrassed to reveal this and the fact that they do not know anything about their birth parents. Another group is comprised of those who lost all or most of their family of origin in some disastrous event or series of happenings like the Holocaust (as was the case of the other reluctant - even horrified - student), war, an earthquake, a hurricane, a flood, a fire, or an airplane crash. The group may not be a safe- and private-enough place for them to do unresolved grief work and deal with the loss of one or two generations of their most significant others, or they may not be ready to deal with the tragedy of multiple losses and inexplicable events.

Thus, it is important to respect resistance and outright refusals. The person can be excused from this particular assignment and invited to pursue it privately with the professor at some time in the future if he or she so chooses. (Interestingly, my students always have - usually within 3 to 9 months.) In a workshop, I indicate that if anyone does not *feel* able to participate, he or she can read something in the compendium while others are drawing, and take from the subsequent discussion whatever is relevant and meaningful without having to do any self-disclosing. This has always sufficed, and no one has ever left the session because of extreme discomfort. Despite these possible exceptions, participation is usually 100%.

Once trainees or patients have depicted their family as they perceive it to be, we explore such questions as:

- Whom did you put down first?
- Do you have any idea why?
- What specific significance does that person have to you at this point in time?

Often participants' eyes will mist or their voices will crack with emotion as old needs and feelings tumble back into consciousness. If they are surprised at their preoccupation with one particular person, we pursue this further:

- What unfinished business do you have with this person that you would like to work through? How might you go about it?

The story of Lisette, which unfolded during the genogramming portion of a workshop in Florida in 1993, will be used to illustrate how the process is likely to evolve.

CASE #3 (Part A)

Lisette was sitting on the center aisle on about the 5th row. She looked startled and tears started to roll down her cheeks. I asked if she wanted to talk about what was happening in her and she nodded "Yes." She stated, "I drew my maternal grandmother (MGM) first although she died when I was 6 years old." Lisette was about 34 or 35 years of age. "She lived with us almost from the time I was born. My dad was in the Navy, and away a great deal. My brother was 5 years older and paid little attention to me. Mom worked full-time and often went out at night with friends to fill her loneliness. Granny was my emotional mom; I could almost smell the cookies she baked and feel her hugs as I remembered her just now. She died suddenly and I was the only one home with her. I was so distraught they wouldn't let me go to the funeral. My whole life changed with her death, and nobody ever dealt with how much I needed granny and what an awful loss it was." As she blurted out her memories, she became increasingly agitated. I asked what she thought might be helpful to her now, stating "It sounds like your granny was very special to you and you never quite thanked her or said goodbye to your satisfaction." Lisette nodded in assent and said, "I guess I'd like to do two things - write a loving farewell letter to my granny and take it to her grave." Then she added, "Maybe I'll find her photo and finally kiss her goodbye." As she said this, she relaxed noticeably and a faint smile of anticipation replaced her tears.

Thus we see that a respondent may select the person who had the most powerful and positive impact on his or her life, such as a grandparent or parent who provided unconditional love, much encouragement, or who was a role model. Conversely, others are preoccupied with someone who they feel disdained, abused, or abandoned them. In exploring this, some reveal an intense wish to find out why they were rejected or betrayed, and some want to "heal the wounds" (Courtois, 1988) or end the "cut-offs" (Bowen, 1978). Still others want retribution or to shut someone totally out of their lives. As the genogram sequence unfolds, questions are raised about what these responses mean to the participants now that they are adults and can process their thoughts and feelings differently than they did in childhood, how they might proceed to implement any choices they might decide to make now vis-à-vis these specific relationships, what the consequences might be for them, and how they anticipate they would react to those consequences. A great deal of self-exploration and soul-searching seems to be evoked. How and why this occurs should become clearer in the following discussion.

CASE #3 (Part B)

Later Lisette said, "It looks like I have some other scores to settle. I now realize how angry I am, underneath this polite façade, at both of my parents and my brother for rarely being there for me. We were superficially the perfect family, pleasant, cordial (Wynne et al., 1958), but oh, so distant. After granny died, I became a latch-key child. My folks thought this was safe since we often lived on a military base and other moms were around to 'keep an eye on me.' We had to behave to make dad look good so he would not be passed over for promotions. I was always compliant and well-behaved while my little heart was breaking - I was so lonely" (F. W. Kaslow, 1993c; F. W. Kaslow & Ridenour, 1984). "We were to follow orders and never break ranks."

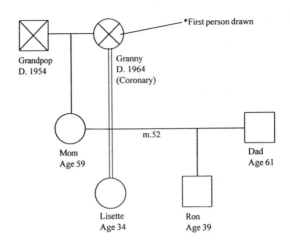

Figure 1. Lisette's Family (1992).

I stated, "Lisette, it sounds like you want to take action and make some modifications in these key relationships. What would you like to tell each of them and what might you indicate you would like in the here-and-now since you really can't change what happened then, only how to use it as a building block now?" She paused and then said, "I'd like to call a family reunion, serve lunch, and for dessert tell them how I felt unwanted and deserted, how I resented them, longed for hugs and attention, and to feel valued. I'd like to lash out in anger and get rid of the pain I carry in my stomach when I talk about my childhood. I'd like them to apologize and acknowledge what they didn't do and then have us reconcile with lots of hugs and a new beginning - where we really see and talk to each other."

Several other workshop participants identified with her anger and said they had experienced similar emotions in the genogramming when they had been told "feel whatever you feel as you draw symbols for the various people you are including," and they remembered their feelings of abandonment and worthlessness.

I gently suggested that Lisette might follow through with her idea, or if she needed assistance, go to a family therapist and jointly plan and "stage" a therapeutic family reunion. She said, "Thanks for validating my feelings; it's a relief to talk about it and be understood. I'll think about how I want to proceed after the workshop is over and I've processed all of my rapidly emerging thoughts and feelings."

Some workshop participants and some patients start with a relative they never met but whose presence in some way permeated or dominated their family of origin. This person's portrait may hang in the living room, or anyone who dishonors the family or violates its traditions may be told, "Your grandmother or grandfather would turn over in their grave if he or she knew what you are doing." At times, the lack of any conversation about an ancestor or current relative may have caused consternation or piqued one's curiosity so they are depicted first. This is the "mystery" person the explorer (person doing genogram) wishes to know more about. One can suggest that eventually they make a voyage home, or if that is not possible, ask questions by phone or letter. I suggest they do this diplomatically and nonconfrontationally, and that to elicit maximum cooperation and information, they couch the requests and queries in terms of a quest to learn more about their roots (Haley, 1976) and their family heritage. It may take weeks or months for the seeds planted to sprout to the point where they are ready to pursue their quest, but many, like Jerry in Case #1, ultimately do.

What has evolved in the years that I have been experimenting with projective genograms is that those who draw themselves first perceive themselves to be doing *their* family, and so to be central to it. In training workshops or in therapy with therapists (F. W. Kaslow, 1984, 1987b), this is a very logical place to begin. The focus at that moment is often on the person of the therapist (in a workshop), and a process of centering has occurred, or is occurring. Although patients may do this for the same reason, it may also reveal extreme self-absorption for narcissistic or other reasons, like a current preoccupation with the need for surgery, a recent job loss, high anxiety about comprehensive exams, or self-centeredness. Because there is no right or wrong place to begin, as no map is externally imposed, all participants are asked why they think they started where they did at this particular moment in time.

In working with trainees in workshops and families in therapy, I give them about 4 to 6 minutes to draw *their* family after the first straightforward instruction. During this time I just sit quietly, observing. Then people listen while each gives an answer to, "With whom did you begin?" and "In retrospect, what does that choice mean to you?" Responses tend to pop out from deep within due to the willingness and ability of many trainees and patients to free-associate to the questions in a safe environment. Individuals are often surprised at their own answers. Frequently tears well up, a lip trembles, or they become downcast as they talk of the person they started with who is now dead and sorely missed. Others become agitated as they recollect and sometimes reexperience anger or a sense of deprivation about what they did not receive that they needed or wanted from a parent (as Lisette in Case #3 did), a grandparent, or a former spouse. Depending on my assessment of how ready and willing they are to begin to deal with what they are revealing and how much they trust me and the others assembled, I will explore further and make some suggestions about how they might acquire information they lack or attempt to reopen and repair a conflictual relationship, or I might recommend other pathways they may consider exploring in the service of the ego (i.e., self-understanding and acceptance). This is exemplified in the preceding sequence with Lisette.

Instead of beginning with the self, people may draw any of the following people first: a maternal or paternal grandparent or great-grandparent, their mother or father, a stepparent, a husband or wife, a former spouse, a brother or sister, a cousin, a son or daughter, a grandchild, a friend or lover. The choice always appears "inevitable," personally meaningful, and right for them. In family therapy sessions, each person in the family may be a little startled to hear where others started, in comparison to their own starting point, and may remark, "I had no idea you felt that way," or "I did not know you were still so upset about that."

Trainees are surprised at the numerous possibilities. Given time and encouragement, they may dialogue with one another.

This can only occur in a context within which it is expected that no one will be criticized, that questions will be asked only to seek clarification, and that there will be no apologies or defensive retorts. What typically emerges is the person's preoccupation with some aspect of the person they drew first. It can be primarily negative or positive; involve enmity or pride; involve worry or joy; involve curiosity or overinvolvement; or evoke numerous other emotions in relation to the person drawn at that moment in time.

Occasionally someone starts with a sibling. If the person is an adult, and the sibling is not acutely ill and therefore not an objective cause of current worry, queries tend to elicit stories of long-term rivalry, resentment over the brother or sister having been the favorite child or the more talented, attractive, chronically ill, and so on. Competitiveness and feelings of somehow being "inferior" often come to the fore. Participants may be preoccupied with ruminating over how to finally prove they are the better child to parents, how to surpass the sibling by earning more money or achieving higher status, or how to transform the childhood rivalry into an adult friendship. When this type of material comes forth, I talk about sibling relationships and may muse over their import given that, when parents die, our siblings are all that is left of our family of origin, and the ties that bind can become more and more meaningful over the years (Bank & Kahn, 1982). I might recommend, if they are receptive to reworking the relationship, that they call the sibling and try to arrange to get together - without parents or spouses - and talk through, as adults, what kind of relationship they would like with one another now and how they can go about co-evolving this. I point out that such sibling reunions can free them in the present from being vulnerable to manipulation from anyone else, and they can build new relationships as adults, laughing and/or crying over the past, ventilating about old feelings, and ultimately letting go of the list of grievances. They may in reminiscing find out for the first time that not only they, but another or all siblings were sexually abused, or that a brother or sister also was distressed by parents' alcoholism, but pretended not to be bothered. They can bond together after such revelations, and may even jointly plan how to create a different atmosphere at future family holiday gatherings and other events.

Sometimes the drawing of a sibling first, particularly by a single adult, can be an expression of a special and enduring friendship. As with all other responses to "who was drawn first," multiple interpretations are possible based on careful observation of facial expressions, posture, gestures, and voice tone, as well as the specific content.

Another popular starting place is one's spouse. This can signify that the person's world revolves around their partner because of love, dependency, domination, or his or her commanding narcissism. Or their mate may be physically or mentally ill and they are worried about his or her health and well-being and their own future. They may be embroiled in great marital strife and be engulfed in thinking about this to the exclusion of almost everything else. As each person present searches for the personal meaning of his or her own depiction and responses, and listens to those of the others assembled, they realize the uniqueness of each one's drawing.

Not all the possible starting points can be elaborated upon here. However, one other starting point is so emotionally significant that it should not go unmentioned. It is important to bear in mind that the age of the participants in a workshop or in therapy will influence the nature of the initial diagramming. Thus, when there are pregnant women or young parents present, more may begin with a child, because this little person may be the central focus of their life. For slightly older parents, a teenager can be pivotal, either because the adult is living vicariously through the adolescent and counting on him or her to fulfill unfulfilled dreams, or because the adolescent is highly rebellious and keeps life chaotic in a dysfunctional family (Olson, Russell, & Sprenkle, 1983). For senior-age parents, continuing concern about an adult child who is still emotionally dependent may lead them to remain focused on this offspring. No matter which of these, or of numerous other possibilities, surface as the basis for the choice, interpretations include comments on perceived dynamics and potential future interactions that can change the nature of discordant, dissatisfying, or turbulent relationships. If child abuse, present or past, is an issue that comes to the fore, appropriate action is taken in therapy and referral suggestions made in workshops.

Throughout the genogramming process, there is attention to issues of chronic physical (Barth, 1993) and mental illness, the special pulls, drains, and stressors these may place on relationships, and the function of these factors in the choice of who was drawn first and why.

Some individuals include in the genogram deceased relatives who were important to them, and others do not. Sometimes those who do include them have not completed the mourning process. For these I may move into a discussion of graveside visits to facilitate closure on grief work (Williamson, 1978), or of having a simulated funeral ceremony as part of a therapy session, using the deceased's photo, to afford an opportunity for saying a different good-bye. Such a dialogue usually has a profound effect as the subject becomes conscious of the longings, hurt, and anger associated with a departed loved one. It is possible that over time, through the therapeutic dialogue, patients may acquire a new way to personally deal with grief and bring to closure an incompletely resolved relationship. On a professional level, trainees absorb awareness of additional techniques which they can incorporate into their clinical practices and use with patients who are confronted by similar dilemmas. After those assembled have had ample time to probe as far as they wish to, they are asked to return to their genogram and include anyone they did not have time to put in earlier.

This portion of the genogramming is drawn to a close when it appears that everyone has finished. In asking participants to analyze their own diagrams, I suggest they consider not only who was drawn and in what order, but the placement of each person's symbol in relation to all the other symbols; how much space/distance separates the different geometric figures, and why; and the size of each symbol - because large versus small may denote power, stature, age, strength, or the lack of same. Given that I do not specify that the squares (□) go on the left and circles (○) go on the right, my patients and trainees arrange themselves and their significant others in accordance with an inner-directed locus of control. They are asked, before we have completed Step One, to include at least three generations.

PROJECTIVE GENOGRAMMING: STEP TWO - WHOM DID YOU OMIT OR EXCLUDE?

Participants are asked to close their eyes for a few seconds, relax, and detach from their family tree. In working with actual patients, if someone appears extremely tense, I might guide them through some relaxation breathing.

In the next sequence, they are asked to open their eyes, look at the genogram with fresh vision, and answer the question, "Whom did you leave out who should have been included?" Quickly, someone may giggle and blurt out such answers as "my stepmother." This is probably the person who most frequently is omitted, usually indicating that she has been emotionally excluded from the respondent's current conceptualizing of "my family." Again we explore: "What does that mean to you or stir up for you?" Usually, they regret that their father married this person and wish she had never come into their life. At this point, they may impulsively disclose why they felt, and still feel, this way; nonetheless, they are free not to pursue the roots of this revelation further.

CASE #3 (Part C)

After several others had disclosed whom they had omitted, to their astonishment or chagrin, and probed the significance of these exclusions, Lisette volunteered, "Wow, for me it's a triple-header . . . With my father away so much, and my mom overly involved with her work and activities, I rarely got to see my dad's folks. They lived far from the (military) bases at which we were stationed. I hardly know them and they are just two more adults in the family who never showed much interest in me . . . and there's my father's second wife (first mention of her existence), whom he married shortly after he was discharged. I didn't put any of these three on."

To a prompting comment gently made to see if she wanted to pursue this further, Lisette said, "Absolutely."

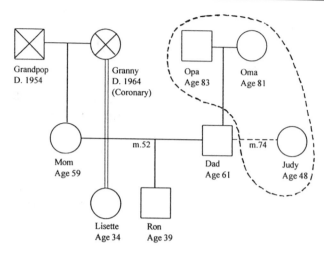

Grouping in circle added in response to query "Whom did you leave off?"

Figure 2. Lisette's Family (1992).

It seemed the floodgates had opened. She shook as she said with a raised voice, "Dad was honorably discharged with high rank, good pay, and good status when I was 16 years old. I thought, I'll finally see my dad every day and maybe we'll be a real family and mom will be here more! Wrong! In a few months, it became clear my parents could not live together full-time. They had each lived such separate lives for so long, and grown in different directions. My hopes were dashed when my dad moved out at the end of 3 months and within a few weeks was living with Judy. I was crushed. They hadn't even filed for divorce. And he lied, saying he had just met her. Can you believe he used to lecture me on acting morally and not embarrassing him? What a double standard!" Lisette asked if we could "understand and empathize with her rage and what hell she had lived through." Everyone nodded. Lisette decided she should add her paternal grandparents and Judy to her genogram, as they were certainly influential in her life. She said, "My head is spinning, so much has been stirred up, but it sure feels like it's time I deal with this mess." She asked if she could think about it overnight and come back on Day #2 of the workshop to consider how she might want to address these residual issues from her earlier life. This was mutually agreed upon.

Sometimes someone spontaneously declares, "I left my in-laws off," and then rationalizes, "You said 'draw my family' and they are part of my spouse's family." Yet it rapidly becomes apparent that others present included their in-laws and that if they are not part of the picture, the children seem to have descended from one set of grandparents only. When they are depicted, what is expressed often is that they like and respect their in-laws and they have strong, positive ties to them. However, on occasion such inclusion signifies preoccupation with overinvolvement in a distressingly negative interaction. Then what usually emerges are often longstanding feelings of nonacceptance, rejection, hostility, enmeshment, and detachment that have not been dealt with or have been dealt with insufficiently. Sometimes the individual completing the genogram was never accepted into the in-law family and has been treated as an outsider or unwelcome interloper for many years. The processing of the preceding experiences may provide the impetus for a voyage home (Bowen, 1978), for holding a family reunion or extended family conference, or, if the individual completing the genogram is in therapy, for a multigenerational family therapy session (Framo, 1981, 1992).

When a former spouse with whom the individual completing the genogram had children has been omitted, here again the children are portrayed as being a descendant of only one parent. Half of the child's biological heritage has been eradicated. When this transpires, it is often helpful to encourage the individual completing the genogram to go back and finish the unresolved trauma of divorce so that children can have access to both parents and can benefit from what each has to offer, without fear that they will be perceived as disloyal, that they will hurt or offend either parent (F. W. Kaslow, 1995; F. W. Kaslow & Schwartz, 1987), or that they will become a scapegoated recipient of some form of retaliation. If 2 or more years have elapsed since the painful parting, a divorce ceremony that acknowledges the positive memories and moves ex-spouses beyond anger and disappointment, could prove to be quite curative and might help them finally achieve a more ego syntonic closure (F. W. Kaslow, 1993a).

Periodically someone blurts out, "I forgot a brother or sister." This is particularly surprising if there have been comments about beginning with a sibling during Step One. Up to this point, these relatives have been very much a part of the "presence" in the room. This makes such an omission even more a projection of the internal reality (i.e., "At least part of me wishes this sibling had never existed"). Occasionally someone adds, "I had forgotten how much I hated, or dreaded, that devil (or a much more pejorative term) for making my life miserable and always getting me into trouble, breaking my toys, stealing my friends, making horrible threats, pushing and/or shoving, and so forth." After finishing this tale of woe, they are asked how they now view this from an adult vantage point, and whether they would like to tell the person how they felt then or to change the nature of their relationship now. If the answer to either of these questions is "Yes," some of the options mentioned earlier are explored.

A didactic presentation of transgenerational influences and loyalties (Bowen, 1978; Boszormenyi-Nagy & Spark, 1973, 1984) is interwoven with or follows the in-depth, profoundly moving experience of working with projective genograms. We shift levels from experiential to theoretical and from personal to professional, always bearing in mind that the participants have contracted for an intensive training experience and not group therapy. There is, however, a commitment to the idea that one becomes most cognizant of theories and techniques by grappling with these experientially (F. W. Kaslow, 1984) in training, in therapy, and in the larger experience of living.

PROJECTIVE GENOGRAMMING: STEP THREE - WHOM WOULD YOU LIKE TO ELIMINATE?

The next series of questions emanates from the core question, "Whom would you like to eliminate?" Amidst startled expressions and anxious laughter, usually a number of people will erase someone. The less inhibited ones present will scribble them out as small children do.

For most, the question provokes some delight at the idea that they could even think about doing this. For others, the idea is disturbing as it touches closely on their innermost and maybe heretofore unspeakable desires. For still a third group, it is inapplicable, and this is stated in the instructions: "Some of you will have no one you want to eliminate, and that's fine." Most frequent on the list of people to be "annihilated" are nasty ex-spouses or in-laws, wicked stepmothers, punitive stepfathers, live-in surrogate parents, and rivalrous siblings. This often leads into self-explorations and revelations of hated or feared significant others.

CASE #4

In a workshop for professionals on "The Self of the Family Therapist" in one of the northeast states in 1993, I demonstrated the use of projective genograms for two main reasons: (a) to enable participants to reexplore their current emotional linkages and legacies, and (b) to introduce them to an additional technique for assessing and treating families. At this juncture in the process, Clyde chortled, "Oh, my God, I left off my first wife, Gail. I drew my biological children (of whom he was the primary residential parent) and my stepchildren (who also resided primarily with him) as if all four were the biological offspring of me and my second wife, Charlene." He expressed amazement at his depiction, and then added, "I drew the family as I really wish it were, even though I know consciously that my ex-wife and her ex-husband still have legal rights. Visits to them are so disruptive, I wish they would vanish, or better yet, had never existed. Charlene is such a great mom, much better than Gail - who abandoned the children - ever was. She was negligent and abusive. Why should she still have 'rights'?"

His voice had suddenly become agitated and louder. Everyone was listening intently. I gently said, "Please don't reveal any more than you feel comfortable telling." He said he wanted to go on - that "It is high time I got back in touch with what I really feel." He went on to say that Charlene's ex was as mean as his ex and as undeserving of his children's love. Charlene's ex paid child support only intermittently, and wreaked havoc whenever he took the children for a day - he didn't want overnights.

He stopped abruptly, let out a deep sigh, and said - "Wow, so that's why I have difficulty working with couples in the throes of divorce. Even though my second marriage is great and in the 3 years we've been together we've all adapted so well, I'm still furious and resentful . . . I guess I do overidentify with the spurned partner and favor sole custody to shared custody arrangements. Why didn't I see this before? I even scoffed when a few clients told me this. How come it didn't get addressed in my individual therapy or in my supervision?"

First, I acknowledged and accepted the angry outburst and commented that it usually takes 2 to 5 years to resolve the fury and reach closure on the divorce. Then, since I'm a firm believer in the concept of readiness, I suggested that he was willing to deal with it now because he was ready to - it was almost 4 years since his divorce and maybe he could move through and beyond anger to some forgiveness and consider the reasons why he had originally loved his ex-wife, and within that perspective, what she had to offer the children. Further, given the contentment he and Charlene shared, perhaps she, too, could reconsider her ex-husband's value to his children. I cautiously recommended they might talk to their ex-spouses and see if they could find a way to enter a more productive phase of living in a post-divorce/remarried family (Ahrons & Rodgers, 1987; F. W. Kaslow, 1993d).

This question often provokes discussions of such emotions as repressed anger, shame, guilt, sorrow, disgust, and humiliation as these feelings resurface toward those persons whose very being infuriates or devastates them. Tales may be told about an in-law who did everything to dissuade a son or daughter from marrying the person of their choice, ostensibly because they were not acceptable based upon some specific difference such as ethnicity, race, religion, or socioeconomic background or because they were perceived as "not good enough," and then were not ever made welcome by an overpossessive, close-knit family that has continued to see and treat them as an intruder. When this has been the scenario and the tug of war has been perpetuated between the son or daughter and his or her in-laws, the desire to have the rejecting or aggressively interfering in-law out of the picture can be very strong. What relief to be able to talk about it in this way, to get the feelings and the struggle out in the open, and then to brainstorm possible new options for coping - maybe for rewriting the family story (O'Hanlon Hudson & Hudson O'Hanlon, 1991) through focusing on solutions (de Shazer, 1985). If some resolution does not occur, the marital discord is likely to resurface, at a minimum, whenever there is a family event or holiday gathering, and to be transmitted to the children who may be pulled inadvertently into the loyalty struggle.

CASE #3 (Part D)

Unable to contain herself, Lisette blurted out, "I'd like to get rid of Judy. She never became my stepmom; instead she completed the process of isolating my dad from me. I scribbled her out, and that helps me see clearly that I want my dad all to myself for a while. I barely know him. Piggybacking on what you have been suggesting to others, I think I'll call him and ask to have lunch together next week. If it goes well, I may then push for dinner once a week - without *her*. I realize now any relationship with Judy can't come 'til dad and I finally get connected." Many assembled nodded, and one said, "Go for it, Lisette. It sounds right on."

Once a workshop or training group hears and sees the volatile and widespread nature of the anger they and some of their colleagues harbor against those expected to be love objects, or at least positively perceived significant others, I shift back to a more generalized and theoretical discussion of hostility in family relationships. This helps to reduce the intensity of the personal reactions and keeps it in the purview of a professional workshop. We may shift to what it is they need to know to treat incestuous (S. Kirschner, D. A. Kirschner, & Rappaport, 1993), violent, and abusive families. Here one can stress that it is a fine line between what "we," the therapists, feel, and what "they," the patients, feel. The universality of anger and enmity is highlighted in an effort to help participants become more empathic with their explosive clients without seeming to condone destructive, hurtful behavior. This phase of the lecture describes how one specific difference between healthy (ostensibly the therapists) and dysfunctional (acting-out patients) people is manifested (Lewis et al., 1976). That is, the healthy person channels anger constructively; releases it in physical activity; or talks about it as a way of communicating it, managing it, and ultimately resolving it. More dysfunctional people have little control over their impulsivity and sometimes the anger explodes and takes the form of child or spouse abuse (Trepper & Barrett, 1989; Walker, 1984), suicide, homicide, or running away and cutting off all contact.

Next, workshop participants are asked to feel and explore their own wellsprings of anger and how they cope with it. They are encouraged to try to identify with the feelings of the abusive, destructive person who seems to have no capacity to channel the rage constructively and, instead, acts out violently. Many participants indicate that they find such people to be their most difficult patients because it is incomprehensible how a father can sexually violate a 2 year old or a mother can intentionally scald a 5 year old in the bathtub. Some participants report months later that this step of the training has given them a much better comprehension of, and empathic ability to work with, abusive patients and other antisocial family members.

PROJECTIVE GENOGRAMMING: STEP FOUR - WHOM WOULD YOU LIKE TO ADD?

The final section of this exploration of unique family bonds and cut-offs revolves around the query:

Whom would you like to add?

The instruction is, "Go ahead and add them. Fulfill your future fantasy family. It can be a specific person or someone in a 'role' or 'category'."

Reactions range from a smile at the expansive prospect to misty eyes over a vacuum experience that cannot be filled. Some want to add a sibling, a spouse, a child, or a grandchild. We may explore how this longing can be actualized, considering many alternatives like verbally agreeing to adopt a friend or cousin in lieu of the missing sibling, seeking a partner through more creative and assertive means than they have heretofore, or rearranging some priorities to have or adopt a child.

CASE #3 (Part E)

At this juncture Lisette looked up with a grin on her face and said mischievously, "After the prior discussions, and my resolve to at least try to square things away with my mom, brother, dad, and maybe eventually Judy, and to make a trip to Michigan to see my grandparents, I think I might finally be able to consider making a commitment to a relationship. Till now I've either turned men off or pushed them away - not allowing anyone to get too close so that if they broke off, I wouldn't feel abandoned again. But another inner voice says I'd like to meet Mr. Right, and he would be trustworthy and loyal. I even added two children, and I guess if I mean it, I have lots of work to do and little time to waste." The person next to her impulsively hugged Lisette and again one could hear encouragement in the form of "Go for it."

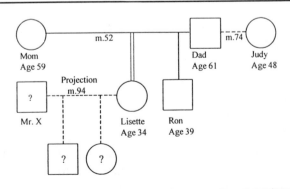

Figure 3. Lisette's Future Fantasy Family (1992).

The question cited previously, "Whom would you like to add?" sometimes evokes a desire to reinsert a parent, grandparent, or sibling who died when they were young and who they therefore never had the opportunity to know. Here again we may do some grief work or suggest ways of making a psychological or physical pilgrimage into one's past (e.g., to talk with those who did know them and might be willing to recount their memories in order to help them reconstruct more about their ancestors and heritage).

When I have been in Israel or Germany training and working with second- and third-generation descendants of Holocaust survivors, both victims (Charny, 1982; Davidson, 1980) and perpetrators (F. W. Kaslow, 1990a), "missing persons" have been a particularly salient feature of projective genogramming. Once these individuals are ready to explore the past and the horrors this journey may unearth, the idea of contacting remaining relations who knew their ancestors is often enthusiastically received. They are encouraged to network with anyone they think might know the whereabouts of long-lost relatives, to return to the hometown in Europe that their family lived in, and to play sleuth: to check Jewish Immigration Agency records (like those of the Hebrew Immigration Aid Society [HIAS]) or even to do a search through the Diaspora Museum at Tel Aviv University. German survivors of perpetrators can follow a similar course of action using comparable sources of information.

These workshops are always highly emotional, with Jewish participants in Israel and elsewhere in the diaspora having to deal with the continuing reality of the enormity of losses from the genocide committed, as well as the international pressures to forgive. Forgetting is impossible; the Holocaust is part of the collective consciousness and unconscious. Today's Germans want to know if, indeed, the sins of the fathers fall onto the children, that is, if they are "born guilty" (Sichrovsky, 1988). Or, as one 30-something fledgling therapist asked me at a workshop conducted near Cologne (Koln), "If my father was a mass murderer, what am I?" They, too, find it difficult to forget this tragic era and forgive their forebears for their inhumanity to their fellow human beings. The projective genogram has proven to be a profound and effective tool for bringing this issue to the fore - something I consider essential because these therapists are treating other victim and perpetrator survivors and are often blocked when it comes to intervening around this core issue.

Those who want a lover, spouse, child, surrogate parent, or sibling have the luxury of adding these and trying to fit themselves into the future context of this new relationship. As they get in touch with their desires and longings, we consider what they can do to "make it happen." Much emphasis is placed on "taking charge of your own life and visualizing your future as you would want it to be," and then brainstorming options to be pursued, like adoption, or a new dating format, as well as assessing what obstacles might crop up in order to foresee ways of overcoming them.

USE OF THE PROJECTIVE GENOGRAM
IN FAMILY BUSINESS CONSULTATION

This section presents a specific example of a kind of psychological practice in which the projective genogram has proven to be a valuable tool for diagnosis and intervention.

During the past decade, I have been engaged in family business consultation (see *Family Business Review,* 1988-1994 for discussions on this specialty), with a particular interest in three aspects of family business: (a) female-owned family businesses, (b) succession planning, and (c) the role of women in male-run or male-dominated family enterprises. Because he is a securities salesman and investment planner, my husband, Solis, sometimes joins me in this consultative work when some of the issues under consideration involve financial planning, investments, capital expansion, and other money matters (F. W. Kaslow & S. Kaslow, 1992). As nearly as we could ascertain at the October 1994 meeting of the Family Firm Institute (FFI), we are one of less than a dozen couples engaged in this type of consultation. In addition, our son, Howard, who is also a stockbroker, sometimes joins us when part of the core dilemma about which we are consulting is intergenerational strife within the context of the business or professional practice. To date, we are unaware of any other two-generation family engaged in a similar endeavor. Perhaps this is the most appropriate place to include a bare-bones, three-generation genogram of my own family as it pertains to our family business heritage and legacy. Siblings of our generation and of our parents'

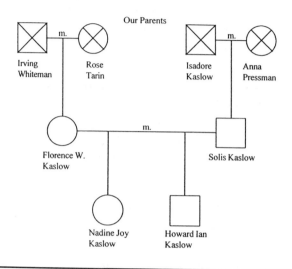

Figure 4. Kaslow Nuclear Family.

generation are not included because they are not relevant to the illustrative purpose of the family tree.

My parents, Irving and Rose Whiteman, both emigrated to this country from Eastern Europe before they were 5 years of age. After they grew up, met, and married here and had two daughters, they went into the grocery business - together - with the living quarters attached to the store for much of my childhood. My husband's parents, Isadore and Anna Kaslow, also emigrated to the United States from Russia when they were very young. They, too, went into a "Mom and Pop" business, only theirs was a dry cleaning store. It also was adjacent to their home. Sol and his sister spent a great deal of time there, helping out in a variety of roles as needed, just as my sister and I did. Our parents worked long hours during our early childhood and young adult years. For example, neighborhood grocery stores often were open from 7:00 a.m. to 10:00 p.m., 6 days a week, and 8:00 a.m. to 2:00 p.m. on Sunday. Fortunately, because these were family businesses on the same premises as our home, we saw a great deal of our two hard-working parents and had a very close and interdependent relationship with them. Our parents had barely survived the arduous, long Depression years of the late 1920s and early 1930s, and so inculcated values of thrift, diligence, perseverance, self-reliance, and family loyalty. My husband and I were both the younger of two children and the only sibling in each family to not only finish college, but go on to graduate school.

We pursued separate careers for the first few decades of our marriage. We have been quite interested in each other's fields and have been supportive of one another's professional activities, accompanying each other to professional events whenever it has been appropriate and feasible. Sol has developed a fine understanding of family dynamics and of many of the major constructs and concepts regarding family structure and functioning. He often quips that he does his own brand of therapy with customers who are upset and angry when the market declines sharply and they experience losses in their portfolio. He has always been concerned when husbands do all of the investing and handle their wives' accounts without the women learning how to manage; he urges both to be involved, and as they grow older, to include their adult children in at least knowing what they have accrued, where it is kept, what the arrangements are for defraying inheritance taxes, and so on. In the same vein, I have learned the language and machinations of the world of finance, acquired an understanding of the complexities of short-term and long-term family financial planning, and gained great respect for the creativity and psychological acumen of those successful businesspeople who abide by ethical principles.

Given that both psychology/family therapy and business/financial/economics-related topics were part of our nightly dinnertime conversation with our children (in addition to "What happened at school, ballet class, band, orchestra, etc.?"), it is probably not surprising that our daughter, Nadine, chose to become a psychologist and family therapist, and our son, Howard, selected a career as a stockbroker. In retrospect, we did not consciously foster these choices, but our children certainly had much exposure to them and liked the interesting, stimulating, multifaceted life-style our careers provided and permitted. Nadine is now chief psychologist in the department of psychiatry at Grady Hospital of Emory University in Atlanta and not directly involved in our family business. However, she and I plus one of her colleagues have recently co-authored a book chapter (N. J. Kaslow, F. W. Kaslow,

& Farber, in press) and are currently under contract to do a book together. In addition, we recently both served as consultants to a family foundation on the topic of where they might invest foundation funds to help stem the tide of what they termed "family disintegration." We had been invited separately by someone who did not know we were related.

Our son actually shares an office with my husband. They have their own partnership within the large New York Stock Exchange firm in which they work. They have separate accounts, yet are familiar enough with each other's accounts to cover for each other with no discontinuity. Their customers know both of them, which enables each of them to have coverage if they want to go out for lunch or take a vacation. They have always maintained an affable and trusting relationship. The future succession plan is clear and mutually agreed upon.

Thus, when I began to receive requests from people running family businesses to consult with them, it seemed natural that my husband and son would become my associates on an "as needed, ad hoc" basis. All of the foregoing has given us an a priori foundation of credibility.

Previously, I have written up a case involving a consultation with a family business owned by a woman whose only offspring, a son, worked for her. Their daily life together was filled with dissension, but they clung to each other because she thought she wanted him ultimately to be her successor, and there was no other relative to benefit from the fruits of her considerable labors. She had emigrated here from Latin America and was very proud of the enormous success she had achieved. Her son did not seem to share her commitment to the ideal of family loyalty; rather he saw the business as a lucrative plum if only he could tolerate her dominating, demanding style. The dance they did was a contentious duel, with matricide threatened whenever the indulged grown son did not get his way, particularly around financial incentives and bonuses (F. W. Kaslow, 1993b).

A similarly dramatic scenario has been present in several cases involving female-owned businesses when the heir apparent was an only child and a son. Coincidentally, in each instance, the woman was left in dire financial straits following a divorce. The child-support payments were either quite meager or not forthcoming, and alimony was either not granted or grossly inadequate. Financially desperate and unskilled, these women took whatever work they could find to "make ends meet." Frequently, the maternal grandmother and friends pitched in to help care for the son as the mother worked excessively long hours. As soon as she learned to navigate the shoals of the business world, each of these women decided that she would focus her ambition and independence on establishing her own business. Based on sheer grit, necessity, perseverance, and determination, each of their businesses became successful. Each of these women also became intrigued with the power and influence she could wield and learned how to play tough in the "big leagues." The son usually apprenticed in the business during their high school and college years, and came to view their mother as a demanding, perfectionistic, and hard-driving woman. Rarely could they measure up to her standards of ambition, commitment to work, or frugality. Usually the sons had been overindulged financially as their mother's business became more profitable; this was her way of assuaging her guilt for neglecting him in terms of time spent together while she was building and running the business.

Doing projective genograms with these women, most of whom had close male associates who were in a somewhat dependent, even parasitic, relationship with them, but whom they would not marry, yielded the following pattern:

Each of these women wanted to add another son who was much more like them; that is, more aggressive, intelligent, striving, and with the business as their main purpose. Each wished her daughter-in-law were warmer and more respectful and appreciative, and that she could have become the daughter the woman had always wanted. Instead, the younger women tended to resent their strong-willed mothers-in-law and felt in competition with her for their husband's time and attention. The sons tended to pick as wives women who wanted homemaking and mothering to be their career to ensure that their children would not be neglected, as they felt they had been. Despite the uneasy truce between these basically incompatible mothers-in-law and daughters-in-law, all wanted the enormous financial perks to be derived from the family business; they counted on the $10,000 a year tax-free gift per family member that never would have happened if mother, as progenitor of the family business, had not been so totally immersed!

One of the commonalities I observed from using and discussing the family projective genogram was that each woman business-owner focused on the grandchildren generation, wanting a grandson in the mold of the son they desired but had not had, and a granddaughter in their own image. If grandchildren already existed, they had selected the one that seemed to most fulfill their longings for a more suitable successor and were doing whatever they could to groom the child and have him or her identify with them. This grandchild became the favorite - the beacon of light for the future. If a granddaughter was the chosen one, a promise was extracted to keep her maiden name if and when she married, so that the family name would live on in and through the business.

Based on the use of the projective genogram in such families, a family conference between mother and son is often very helpful. After some of the areas of conflict around thwarted expectations, personality clashes, and divergent goals are resolved by focusing on shared objectives, loyalty bonds, and the financial gains to be derived by working more harmoniously, as well as by establishing clearer job descriptions, promotion guidelines, and compensation schedules, the family conferences are expanded to include the daughter-in-law and, eventually, the teenage children. Family members may be encouraged to set up a family foundation to unite them around a philanthropic cause that has significance for them across generations. Questions about what the family members value from their heritage and what they wish to transmit through the family business to successive generations are often common themes of these meetings. If these intergenerational conflicts are not resolved, it is likely that the business will be sold and the next generation will lose much of its potential inheritance and earning capacity.

In larger family businesses, such as a family business begun by three brothers, which grows into a fairly large corporation over a period of 30 to 40 years, severe problems often arise when the now senior members of the firm begin to think seriously about retiring. Often they have invested so much of their time, money, and energy in the business that their sense of self is an integral part of their workaday world. The thought of relinquishing control may be onerous to one brother, and may evoke ambivalence in the other brothers, as they ponder retirement. In addition to the fears that accompany a less structured existence and loss of prominence as a Chief Executive Officer (CEO or Corporate President, or Vice-President of an International Division), they are often beset by worries about which of their many children is apt to be the best successor and how to avoid a battle between the three branches of the now extended family.

Doing succession planning is a complex, intricate process. It often takes several years for an orderly succession to occur: from the commencing of the process of contemplating retirement, through determining what are thought to be the qualities and characteristics most predictive of success in the next CEO; to going through the search and selection process in the fairest, most constructive, and ethical manner; to informing the other brothers and their wives of the choice; to telling the chosen one he or, increasingly, she has been designated and informing the other contenders of their projected future involvement in the company so they stay in the firm and do not become disaffected or jealous; and finally to mentoring one's successor so that he or she is readied to assume the reins when the predetermined time for the transfer of power arrives.

I have found the use of the projective genogram to be a valuable strategy for helping such CEOs determine what they are seeking in a successor. It enables them to explore the past and reconsider what they most treasured in the legacy they derived from their grandparents and parents. It invites reaffirmation of the strong bonds between them and their siblings and the exciting, rewarding years they spent together establishing and expanding their business from the kernel of an idea to a mammoth enterprise. It encourages acknowledgement of the contributions to and sacrifices made for the welfare of the businesses by the spouses and the children. It affords an opportunity to examine the nature of their multiple family relationships and to consider what kind of legacy they want to have for their grandchildren, as well as which of their sons, daughters, nieces, or nephews is most likely to be able to fulfill the CEO's and their own dreams for the future. It is about past, present, and future - about continuity across time and space. Writing a family mission statement that incorporates the values of the larger family and how these are to be given expression through the family business and its other enterprises - such as its foundation or other philanthropic wing - might also be encouraged. As they work with the projective genogram, expressing their fears and hopes for the future and the direction in which they would like the family business to move, greater clarity is often achieved about which of three or four candidates for CEO will be the best choice. And because strong leadership qualities can be evidenced by men and women alike, the selection process is less linked to gender than in earlier times.

Once their projective genograms seem complete, the CEO and all of those in the small consultation group can be asked where they see those included on the genogram who are already working in the family firm, as well as those who have expressed an interest in doing so, fitting into specific slots in the company. In a way, one diagram can be used as an overlay on the other. Where there are positions to be filled and no one on the horizon suited for those jobs, the question, "Whom would you like to add?" takes the discussion in the direction of when it is important to add non-family members to the team and how they ultimately can be integrated into the company so they do not feel like outsiders.

This section has described the use of projective genograms outside the more usual context of family therapy or the training of family therapists. Hopefully this technique may be adopted by other family business consultants, when appropriate, and by family therapists or consultants in other organizational settings.

THE FINALE AND
POSSIBLE EPILOGUES

One objective of a workshop involving projective genogramming is to help people think in terms of their historic personal past and what needs to be accomplished with members of their family of origin in order to work through prior relationship impasses and to make family relationships more fulfilling in the present, as well as to steer clear of those family relationships that remain unchanging and distressing so as not to get pulled back into the dysfunctional interactions they have tried so hard to escape and grow beyond. A second objective is to help people conceive of their present and future interpersonal relationship system as something they can continue to construct, melding family of origin and family of procreation, if they choose to have one, in a meaningful way. The projective genogram invites them to find the emotional energy to optimistically pursue the kinds of relationships they wish to have today and tomorrow.

Usually we end with a summary of the salient concepts in family therapy/psychology (F. W. Kaslow, 1990b) which undergird work on family-of-origin issues and genogramming. These are drawn primarily from psychodynamic approaches (Ackerman, Beatman, & Sherman, 1961), object relations approaches (Slipp, 1988), Bowenian systems theory (Bowen, 1978; Friedman, 1985; Gerson & McGoldrick, 1986; McGoldrick & Gerson, 1985), relational/contextual therapy (Boszormenyi-Nagy & Spark, 1973, 1984), and other multigenerational and family-of-origin therapies (Framo, 1981, 1992). Thoughts about family games and how these can be untangled are derived from Prata (1990), while ideas on restructuring have their roots in structural family therapy (Minuchin & Fishman, 1981). This broad theoretical perspective is integrative, or dialectic, as I call it (F. W. Kaslow, 1981, 1993b); it allows maximum freedom for participants to free-associate to the questions. Long-obscured memories often resurface. Usually all present agree that this personal projective exploration constitutes a powerful way to bring about the return of repressed feelings and memories and enables them to chart their own relational future.

This technique emanated from the ideas of traditional genogramming summarized by McGoldrick and Gerson (1985), and takes the ideas for genogram construction and interpretation into new terrain. It fosters both the external journey to recreate one's biological historical past *and* the internal journey to process one's emotions about the connections to relatives and one's own place and role in the extended family system.

Workshop participants are invited to contact me if they want to process privately what has been stirred up, because I believe we must be available in this way when we have ventured into this type of emotional terrain and engaged in the utilization of such provocative techniques.

APPENDIX:
GENOGRAM FORMAT*

A. Symbols to Describe Basic Family Membership and Structure. (Include on genogram significant others who lived with or cared for family members - place them on the right side of the genogram with a notation about who they are.)

Male: ☐   Female: ○   Birth Date ⟶ 43-75 ⟵ Death Date

Death = X

Index Person (IP) or Identified Patient: ☐ ◎

Marriage (give date; husband on left, wife on right): m.60

Living Together Relationship or Liaison: 72

Marital Separation (give date): s.70

Divorce (give date): d.72

Children (list in birth order, beginning with oldest on left): 60 62 65

Adopted or Foster Children:
adopted   foster

Fraternal Twins:

Identical Twins:

Pregnancy:
3 mos.

Spontaneous Abortion:

Induced Abortion:

Stillbirth:

Members of Current IP Household (circle them):

---

*Note. From "Constructing and Interpreting Genograms: The Example of Sigmund Freud's Family" by R. Gerson and M. McGoldrick in *Innovations in Clinical Practice: A Source Book* (Vol. 5, p. 207), by P. A. Keller and L. G. Ritt (Eds.), 1986, Sarasota, FL: Professional Resource Exchange, Inc. Copyright © 1986 by Professional Resource Exchange, Inc. Reprinted by permission.

Projective Genogramming

Where changes in a child's living arrangements have occurred, please note:

B.   Family Interaction Patterns. The following symbols are among the least precise information on the genogram, but can be key indicators of relationship patterns the clinician wants to remember:

Very Close Relationship:

Conflictual Relationship:

Emotionally Distant Relationship:

Estrangement or Cut-Off (give dates if possible):

Cut-Off
62-78

C.   Medical History. Since the genogram is meant to be an orienting map of the family, there is room to indicate only the most important factors. Thus, list only major illnesses or chronic medical problems. Include dates in parentheses where feasible or applicable. Use *DSM-IV* categories or recognized abbreviations where available (e.g., cancer: CA; stroke: CVA).

D.   Other Family Information should, when appropriate, be noted on the genogram with dates, if possible.

1. Ethnic Background
2. Religion or Religious Change
3. Education
4. Occupation or Unemployment
5. Trouble with Law
6. Physical Abuse or Incest
7. Obesity or Anorexia
8. Dates When Family Members Left Home: LH '74
9. Current Location of Family Members

E.   Alcohol or Drug Abuse. Please darken top half of square or circle and give dates.

F.   Other Key Information. This would include anniversary dates, concurrent events, nodal events, changes in the family constellation since the genogram was made, hypotheses, and other notations of major family issues or changes. These notations should always be dated, and should be kept to a minimum, since every extra piece of information on a genogram complicates it and therefore diminishes its readability.

REFERENCES

Ackerman, N. W., Beatman, F. L., & Sherman, S. N (1961). *Exploring the Base of Family Therapy.* New York: Family Service Association of America.

Ahrons, C. R., & Rodgers, R. H. (1987). *Divorced Families: A Multi-Disciplinary Developmental View.* New York: W. W. Norton.

Bank, S. R., & Kahn, M. D. (1982). *The Sibling Bond.* New York: Basic Books.

Barth, J. (1993). *It Runs in My Family: Overcoming the Legacy of Family Illness.* New York: Brunner/Mazel.

Boszormenyi-Nagy, I., & Spark, G. (1973). *Invisible Loyalties.* New York: Harper & Row.

Boszormenyi-Nagy, I., & Spark, G. (1984). *Invisible Loyalties.* New York: Brunner/Mazel.

Bowen, M. (1978). *Family Therapy in Clinical Practice.* New York: Jason Aronson.

Carter, E., & McGoldrick, M. (Eds.). (1980). *The Family Life Cycle.* New York: Gardner.

Charny, I. W. (1982). *How Can We Commit the Unthinkable? Genocide: The Human Cancer.* Boulder, CO: Westview Press.

Courtois, C. A. (1988). *Healing the Incest Wounds: Adult Survivors in Therapy.* New York: W. W. Norton.

Davidson, S. (1980). The clinical effects of massive psychic trauma in families of holocaust survivors. *Journal of Marital and Family Therapy, 6,* 11-22.

de Shazer, S. (1985). *Keys to Solution in Brief Therapy.* New York: W. W. Norton.

Family Business Review. (1988-1994). San Francisco, CA: Jossey Bass.

Fay, A., & Lazarus, A. (1984). The therapist in behavioral and multi-modal therapy. In F. W. Kaslow (Ed.), *Psychotherapy With Psychotherapists* (pp. 1-18). New York: Haworth.

Framo, J. L. (1981). The integration of marital therapy with sessions with the family of origin. In A. S. Gurman & D. P. Kniskern (Eds.), *Handbook of Family Therapy* (pp. 133-158). New York: Brunner/Mazel.

Framo, J. L. (1992). *Family of Origin Therapy: An Intergenerational Approach.* New York: Brunner/Mazel.

Friedman, E. H. (1985). *Generation to Generation: Family Process in Church and Synagogue.* New York: Guilford.

Gerson, R., & McGoldrick, M. (1986). Constructing and interpreting genograms: The example of Sigmund Freud's family. In P. A. Keller & L. G. Ritt (Eds.), *Innovations in Clinical Practice: A Source Book* (Vol. 5, pp. 203-220). Sarasota, FL: Professional Resource Exchange.

Goldstein, J., Freud, A., & Solnit, A. J. (1973). *Beyond the Best Interests of the Child.* New York: Free Press.

Guerin, P. J. (1976). Family therapy: The first twenty-five years. In P. J. Guerin (Ed.), *Family Therapy and Practice* (pp. 2-22). New York: Garden Press.

Guerin, P. J., & Fogarty, T. (1972). Study your own family. In A. Ferber, M. Mendelsohn, & A. Napier (Eds.), *The Book of Family Therapy* (pp. 445-467). New York: Science House.

Haley, A. (1976). *Roots.* Garden City, NY: Doubleday.

Herz-Brown, F. (1991). *Reweaving the Family Tapestry.* New York: W. W. Norton.

Imber-Black, E., Roberts, J., & Whiting, R. (1988). *Rituals in Families and Family Therapy.* New York: W. W. Norton.

Kaslow, F. W. (1981). A diaclectic approach to family therapy and practice: Selectivity and synthesis. *Journal of Marital and Family Therapy, 7,* 345-351.

Kaslow, F. W. (1982). History of family therapy in the United States: A kaleidoscopic overview. In F. W. Kaslow (Ed.), *The International Book of Family Therapy* (pp. 5-40). New York: Brunner/Mazel.

Kaslow, F. W. (Ed.). (1984). *Psychotherapy With Psychotherapists.* New York: Haworth.

Kaslow, F. W. (1986). An intensive training experience: A six day post graduate institute model. *Journal of Psychotherapy and the Family, 1,* 73-82.

Kaslow, F. W. (1987a). Marital and family therapy. In M. B. Sussman & S. K. Steinmetz (Eds.), *Handbook of Marriage and the Family* (pp. 835-859). New York: Plenum.

Kaslow, F. W. (Ed.). (1987b). *The Family Life of Psychotherapists.* New York: Haworth.

Kaslow, F. W. (1990a). Treating holocaust survivors. *Contemporary Family Therapy, 12,* 393-405.

Kaslow, F. W. (Ed.). (1990b). *Voices in Family Psychology* (Vols. 1 & 2). Newbury Park, CA: Sage.

Kaslow, F. W. (1993a). The divorce ceremony: A healing strategy. In T. Nelson & T. Trepper (Eds.), *101 Interventions in Family Therapy* (pp. 341-345). New York: Haworth.

Kaslow, F. W. (1993b). The lore and lure of family business. *American Journal of Family Therapy, 21,* 3-16.

Kaslow, F. W. (Ed.). (1993c). *The Military Family in Peace and War.* New York: Springer.

Kaslow, F. W. (1993d). Understanding and treating the remarriage family. In *Directions in Marriage and Family Therapy, 1*(3), 1-16. (New York: Hatherleigh Co.)

Kaslow, F. W. (1995). Dynamics of divorce therapy. In R. H. Mikesell, D. D. Lusterman, & S. H. McDaniel (Eds.), *Family Psychology and Systems Theory.* Washington, DC: American Psychological Association.

Kaslow, F. W., & Friedman, J. (1977). Utilization of family photos and movies in family therapy. *Journal of Marriage and Family Therapy, 3,* 19-25.

Kaslow, F. W., & Kaslow, S. (1992). The family that works together: Special problems of family businesses. In S. Zedeck

(Ed.), *Work, Families and Organizations* (pp. 312-351). San Francisco, CA: Jossey Bass.

Kaslow, F. W., & Ridenour, R. I. (Eds.). (1984). *The Military Family: Dynamics and Treatment.* New York: Guilford.

Kaslow, F. W., & Schwartz, L. L. (1987). *Dynamics of Divorce.* New York: Brunner/Mazel.

Kaslow, N. J., Kaslow, F. W., & Farber, E. W. (in press). Theories and techniques of marital and family therapy. In M. B. Sussman & S. K. Steinmetz (Eds.), *Handbook of Marriage and the Family.* New York: Plenum.

Kerr, M., & Bowen, M. (1988). *Family Evaluation.* New York: W. W. Norton.

Kirschner, S., Kirschner, D. A., & Rappaport, R. (1993). *Working With Adult Incest Survivors.* New York: Brunner/Mazel.

Lewis, J., Beavers, W. R., Gossett, J. T., & Phillips, V. A. (1976). *No Single Thread: Psychological Health and the Family System.* New York: Brunner/Mazel.

McGoldrick, M., & Gerson, R. (1985). *Genograms in Family Assessment.* New York: W. W. Norton.

Minuchin, S., & Fishman, H. C. (1981). *Family Therapy Techniques.* Cambridge, MA: Harvard University Press.

O'Hanlon Hudson, P., & Hudson O'Hanlon, W. (1991). *Rewriting Love Stories.* New York: W. W. Norton.

Olson, D. H., Russell, C., & Sprenkle, D. H. (1983). Circumplex model VI: Theoretical update. *Family Process, 22,* 69-83.

Prata, G. (1990). *A Systemic Harpoon into Family Games.* New York: Brunner/Mazel.

Sichrovsky, P. (1988). *Born Guilty.* New York: Basic Books.

Slipp, S. (1988). *The Technique and Practice of Object Relations in Family Therapy.* New York: Jason Aronson.

Trepper, T. S., & Barrett, M. J. (1989). *Systemic Treatment of Incest: A Therapeutic Handbook.* New York: Brunner/Mazel.

Walker, L. E. A. (1984). *The Battered Woman Syndrome.* New York: Springer.

Walker, L. E. A. (1989). *Terrifying Love.* New York: Harper & Row.

Weiser, J. (1993). *Photo Therapy Techniques.* San Francisco: Jossey Bass.

Williamson, D. S. (1978). New life at the graveyard: A method of therapy for individuation from a dead former parent. *Journal of Marriage and Family Counseling, 4,* 93-101.

Wynne, L., Ryckoff, I., Day, J., & Hirsch, S. H. (1958). Pseudo-mutuality in schizophrenia. *Psychiatry, 21,* 205-220.

If You Found This Book Useful . . .

You might want to know more about our other titles.

If you would like to receive our latest catalog, please return this form:

Name:_____
(Please Print)

Address:_____

Address:_____

City/State/Zip:_____

Telephone:(_____)_____

I am a:

_____ Psychologist	_____ Mental Health Counselor
_____ Psychiatrist	_____ Marriage and Family Therapist
_____ School Psychologist	_____ Not in Mental Health Field
_____ Clinical Social Worker	_____ Other:_____

◆ ◆ ◆

Professional Resource Press
P.O. Box 15560
Sarasota, FL 34277-1560

Telephone #941-366-7913
FAX #941-366-7971

Add A Colleague To Our Mailing List . . .

If you would like us to send our latest catalog to one of your colleagues, please return this form.

Name:_____
(Please Print)

Address:_____

Address:_____

City/State/Zip:_____

Telephone:(_____)_____

I am a:

_____ Psychologist	_____ Mental Health Counselor
_____ Psychiatrist	_____ Marriage and Family Therapist
_____ School Psychologist	_____ Not in Mental Health Field
_____ Clinical Social Worker	_____ Other:_____

◆　　　◆　　　◆

Professional Resource Press
P.O. Box 15560
Sarasota, FL 34277-1560

Telephone #941-366-7913
FAX #941-366-7971